PAKISTAN
the land

Carolyn Black

A Bobbie Kalman Book

The Lands, Peoples, and Cultures Series

Crabtree Publishing Company

The Lands, Peoples, and Cultures Series

Created by Bobbie Kalman

Coordinating editor
Ellen Rodger

Production coordinator
Rosie Gowsell

Project development, photo research, design, and editing
First Folio Resource Group, Inc.
  Erinn Banting
  Tom Dart
  Greg Duhaney
  Söğüt Y. Güleç
  Jaimie Nathan
  Debbie Smith

Prepress and printing
Worzalla Publishing Company

Consultants
Dr. Naeem Ahmed, Vice Consul, Consulate General of Pakistan, Toronto; David Butz, Department of Geography, Brock University; Nancy Cook; Tahira Naqvi, Westchester Community College and New York University; Dr. Naren Wagle, Center for South Asian Studies, University of Toronto

Photographs
Mary Altier: p. 21 (right); AP/Wide World Photos: p. 11 (both); Piers Benatar/Panos Pictures: p. 12 (left); David Butz: cover; Giles Calidicott/Axiom Photographic Agency: p. 28 (left); Corbis/Magma Photo News, Inc.: p. 16 (top); Corbis/Magma Photo News, Inc./David Cumming, Eye Ubiquitous: p. 20 (right); Corbis/Magma Photo News, Inc./ Tania Midgley: p. 31; Corbis/Magma Photo News, Inc./ Christine Osborne: p. 3; Corbis/Magma Photo News, Inc./ Galen Rowell: p. 6 (left); Corbis/Magma Photo News, Inc./Nik Wheeler: p. 17 (left); Christine Dameyer: p. 4 (right), p. 19 (left); A.J. Deane/Bruce Coleman Inc.: p. 13 (bottom); Ric Ergenbright: p. 23 (left); Sarah Errington/Hutchison Library: p. 20 (left); Robert Harding: p. 5 (left), p. 13 (top), p. 29; Juliet Highet/Hutchison Library: p. 9 (bottom); Jim Holmes/Axiom Photographic Agency: p. 6 (right); Javed A. Jafferji/Panos Pictures: p. 4 (left), p. 18 (top); Ed Kashi: p. 21 (left), p. 26 (both), p. 27 (bottom), p. 28 (right); John King/ Lonely Planet Images: p. 17 (right); Paolo Koch/Robert Harding: p. 8; Paolo Koch/Photo Researchers: p. 18 (right); Tom & Pat Leeson/Photo Researchers: p. 30 (left); Tom McHugh/Photo Researchers: p. 30 (right); Sarah Murray: p. 5 (bottom); Christine Osborne: p. 12 (right), p. 14 (top), p. 15 (both), p. 16 (bottom), p. 19 (right), p. 22 (both), p. 23 (right), p. 24 (top); Galen Rowell: p. 7; Scala/Art Resource: p. 19 (right); Chris Stowers/Panos Pictures: p. 25 (right); Trip/M. Barlow: p. 23 (right); Trip/E. Rogers: p. 14 (bottom); Trip/H. Rogers: p. 9 (top); Trip/Trip: p. 25 (left); Brian A. Vikander: p. 10

Map
Jim Chernishenko

Illustrations
Dianne Eastman: icon
David Wysotski, Allure Illustrations: back cover

Cover: In the Hoper Valley, Gilgit District, Northern Areas, apricot trees come into blossom in the spring. By late summer, rooftops will be covered with the fruit as it dries in the sun.

Icon: Tall mountain ranges, such as the Karakoram Mountains which appear at the head of each section, tower throughout northern Pakistan. Many climbers think that the mountain K2, in the Karakoram Range, is the most difficult mountain in the world to climb.

Title page: Nomadic people travel by camel through the Bolan Pass, in the western province of Baluchistan. Baluchistan is so dry and barren that some people move from place to place to find good sources of food and water.

Back cover: The Indus River dolphin is one of the few freshwater dolphins in the world, and it lives only in Pakistan. This species of dolphin swims on its side, which allows it to live in shallow parts of the Indus River.

Published by
Crabtree Publishing Company

PMB 16A,	612 Welland Avenue	73 Lime Walk
350 Fifth Avenue	St. Catharines	Headington
Suite 3308	Ontario, Canada	Oxford OX3 7AD
New York	L2M 5V6	United Kingdom
N.Y. 10118		

Cataloging-in-Publication Data
Black, Carolyn.
  Pakistan. The land / Carolyn Black.
    p. cm. -- (Lands, peoples, and cultures series)
  Includes index.
  Summary: Text and photographs portray Pakistan's geography and climate, city and rural life, industry, and transportation.
    ISBN 0-7787-9346-X (RLB) -- ISBN 0-7787-9714-7 (pbk.)
    1. Pakistan--Juvenile literature. [1. Pakistan.] I. Title. II. Series.
    DS376.9 .B55 2003
    954.91--dc21
                                              2002013728
                                              LC

Contents

Karachi, on the shore of the Arabian Sea, is Pakistan's largest city. More than seven million people live there.

A young shepherd holds his goat at the edge of the Karakoram Highway. The highway is built on top of the Silk Road, an ancient trade route that linked Roman and Chinese civilizations.

Pakistan lies along the western part of the Indian **subcontinent**. It is a dry land, with large stretches of mud-cracked plains, dusty **plateaus**, and deserts. Some of the highest mountains in the world rise in the north, with mountain passes winding between their rocky sides. The Indus River rushes down from the mountains and flows the length of the country. For the past 8,000 years, this river has been a source of life for Pakistan's people, animals, and farmland.

Facts at a glance

Official name: Islamic Republic of Pakistan
Area: 307,295 square miles
  (796,100 square kilometers)
Population: 140 million
Capital: Islamabad
Languages: English (official), Urdu (national)
Main religion: Islam
Currency: Pakistani rupee
National holiday: Pakistan Day
  (March 23)

A young country

Although people have lived in the land we now call Pakistan for thousands of years, it did not become a country until 1947, when it split away from India to form its own nation. Pakistan is divided into four provinces — the North-West Frontier Province in the northwest, Punjab, or Panjab, in the central east, Sind in the southeast, and Baluchistan in the west. The Federally Administered Northern Areas, in the northeast, are also governed by Pakistan, although they are not a province.

When Pakistan separated from India, both countries wanted to control the region of Jammu and Kashmir, near the northeast tip of Pakistan. A war broke out and, eventually, the region was divided between the two countries. Pakistan and India still disagree over which country should control Jammu and Kashmir, and battles sometimes break out between the two countries' armies.

The Takht-i-Bahi monastery, in the north, was once home to monks, or religious men, who devoted their lives to the study of the Buddhist religion.

Cousins from the Hunza Valley, in the north, enjoy warm summer weather.

The Indus River begins in mountains in the country of Tibet, just north of Pakistan, and flows for 1,700 miles (2,700 kilometers). It rushes into northern Pakistan as a narrow **torrent**. In the center of the country, the river slows down and spreads out, becoming more than ten miles (sixteen kilometers) wide in some places. Large water buffalo splash along its shores, and palm trees grow on parts of its low banks. The river ends its journey in the south of Pakistan, where it runs into the Arabian Sea. At its mouth, it passes through a river **delta** filled with **lagoons** and swamps with **mangrove trees**.

The Indus River is the longest river in Pakistan.

Northern mountains

Four enormous mountain ranges meet in northern Pakistan — the Himalaya, Karakoram, Pamir, and Hindu Kush. The Himalayas stretch across South Asia, forming the world's highest mountain range. The peaks in this range include Nanga Parbat. At 26,660 feet (7,998 meters), Nanga Parbat is the ninth highest mountain in the world. Its name, which means "naked mountain" in the language of the Kashmiri people, refers to its bare south side. That side is so steep that snow, which covers the rest of the mountain, cannot stick to it.

Long lines of slow-moving ice, called glaciers, run down the sides of Pakistan's mountains. Pakistan has more, and longer, glaciers than any land outside the North and South Poles. Its three most famous glaciers run through the Karakoram Range: the Siachen, the Batura, and the 55-mile- (88-kilometer-) long Baltoro. Scattered between the glaciers are forts built by the rulers of ancient mountain kingdoms. The forts of Altit and Baltit, in the Karakoram Range, are both more than 750 years old.

A climber crosses glaciers in the Braldu Gorge, in the Karakoram Range.

Still rising

More than 130 million years ago, most of Pakistan, as well as India, was not connected to the rest of Asia. They were on a separate piece of land, called the Indian Plate. The rest of Asia was on the Asian Plate. About 130 million years ago, the Indian Plate started moving north toward the Asian Plate. About 50 million years ago, the two plates collided. The land crumpled and buckled, forming high mountains in the north of Pakistan. Even today, the Indian Plate is moving north about two inches (five centimeters) a year. Nanga Parbat is being squeezed up because of the pressure, rising by .28 inches (7 millimeters) every year.

Many of the rocky cliffs in the Karakoram Mountains are shades of black and brown. **Kara** *means "black" in the Turkish language.*

Climbing to the clouds

Pakistan's high mountains attract climbers from all over the world. Scaling the sides of these mountains is exciting, but dangerous. Many people have died while trying to ascend mountains such as Nanga Parbat, which is nicknamed "Killer Mountain."

A favorite challenge for climbers is the mountain K2. It was named K2 because it was the second peak to be measured in the Karakoram Range. K2 is the second highest mountain in the world. It towers 28,250 feet (8,475 meters), only 778 feet (233 meters) lower than Mount Everest. Many climbers consider K2 harder to conquer than Mount Everest because it is so steep and icy, and sudden avalanches bury unlucky climbers. Some Pakistanis in the area earn a living by leading expeditions up the rough slopes or carrying climbers' equipment.

Mountain passes

When people in Pakistan want to cross the mountains, they often travel through passes. These narrow passages connect places within Pakistan, and connect Pakistan to other countries. Trains run through some passes but many travelers walk or ride camels, yaks, or donkeys through them. Their journeys often take days.

The most famous pass, the Khyber Pass, links Pakistan to Afghanistan, the country to its west. The Khyber Pass twists and turns through the rough Hindu Kush Mountains for more than 33 miles (53 kilometers). Farther north, the Lowari Pass winds through mountain forests between the Chitral Valley and the town of Dir. This pass is closed in the winter because heavy snow makes it difficult to cross.

Two roads pass through the Khyber Pass: one for motor traffic and one for traditional caravans, or groups of people traveling with animals. At its narrowest point, the Khyber Pass is only 98 feet (30 meters) wide.

The land of five rivers

After the Indus River leaves the mountains in the north, it flows south and passes into the province of Punjab. Punjab means "land of five rivers." It is here that the Indus is joined by four other rivers, or its **tributaries**: the Chenab, Jhelum, Ravi, and Sutlej. Its fifth tributary, the Beas, runs through India. The five rivers keep most of Punjab and the northern parts of Sind green. This **fertile** land, which makes up one-third of Pakistan, is known as the Indus Plain. Most Pakistanis live on the plain, and farmers grow most of the country's food in its fields.

Away from the river

Lying to the west of the fertile Indus Plain is the dry and dusty province of Baluchistan. Baluchistan is the largest province in Pakistan, but has the fewest people. The soil is sandy and too dry for growing most crops. Without water from major rivers, it is difficult to farm or build large industries.

Stretching over the western part of the province is the Baluchistan Plateau, a flat, rocky area with little plant life. Mountains rise to the north and west of the plateau. Some mountains have long, narrow cracks called *tangis*, which appear after earthquakes. Deep *tangis* sometimes run all the way through mountains. People can walk through the widest cracks, from one side of the mountain to the other.

A boy walks over sand dunes in the Thar Desert. There is so little water in the desert that almost no trees or vegetation grow.

Thar Desert

East of Sind's fertile plains lies the burning sand of the Tharparkar, or Thar Desert. The Thar Desert also reaches into eastern Punjab, where it becomes the Cholistan Desert, and into northwest India. The Thar Desert is the largest desert on the Indian subcontinent, measuring 11,200 square miles (29,000 square kilometers). Very few people live among its stretches of shifting sand, sand dunes, and gravel plains.

The Swat River, in the north, tumbles down from snow-capped mountains into a valley filled with wildflowers, bushes, and trees.

Strong winds blow spirals and clouds of dust in the Shigar Valley, in the Karakoram Mountains. Large dust storms block out sunlight, and often cause the temperature to drop quickly.

The weather in Pakistan is different depending on what part of the country you are in and how high up you are. Summer temperatures all over are hot, except in the mountains where snow covers the highest peaks year round. Temperatures in the center of the country reach 110° Fahrenheit (43° Celsius). In the winter, the south is warmer than the north, where temperatures can drop to 4° Fahrenheit (–16° Celsius).

Rainstorms

Very little rain falls in Pakistan. The country's average rainfall is only 10 inches (25 centimeters) per year. Most of the rain falls in the northern mountains and on the fertile plains of Punjab from July until September. During this season, winds called monsoons carry moisture from the Indian Ocean over Pakistan, dumping it on the land as heavy rain. The southwest has the least amount of rain and sometimes experiences droughts, which are long periods when very little or no rain falls. During droughts, crops are destroyed and people are forced to move to other parts of the country in search of food and water.

Sandstorms

Strong winds sweeping across the Thar Desert and parts of Baluchistan create huge spirals of dust and sand. In May and June, the air in the Thar Desert can become so thick with wind-driven sand that people cannot see the sun. In Baluchistan, a scorching summer wind called the *juloh*, which means "flame," kills even the toughest desert plants.

Floods

Heavy rains during monsoon season cause Pakistan's rivers to rise and flood the land. Flooding also occurs when a glacial dam bursts. Glacial dams happen when a glacier crosses a river and glacial meltwater pools into a lake. The dam bursts after extreme melting or glacial pressure. Areas that are regularly flooded are called floodplains. The Ravi River, in Punjab, frequently overflowed onto its floodplains until the 1960s, when embankments, or walls, were built along the sides of the river. The embankments, which are made from rocks and cement, hold water inside the river's banks.

A family carries bundles of belongings away from their flooded home in Biden, a town east of Karachi.

Damage from floods

In September 1992, two weeks of heavy monsoon rains in Punjab and Sind caused Pakistan's worst floods in more than 100 years. Thousands of people died, more than a million were left homeless, and crops along the Indus River were ruined. To save large cities from being flooded, the government ordered people to destroy some embankments, allowing water to escape onto surrounding farmland before it reached the cities. This saved the cities, but flooded even more crops, as well as small villages.

An earthquake in 2001 caused the roofs of these buildings in the southeastern city of Hyderabad to collapse. The earthquake was so strong that it was also felt in India, Bangladesh, and Nepal.

Sindhis

People who live in Sind and speak Sindhi are called Sindhis. Like Punjabis, many of them grow crops on land watered by the Indus. Sindhis who live in rural areas practice traditional Sindhi customs, which include celebrating the wrestling festival of *Malkhara* and making blue and white pottery.

Young Punjabi men from Rawalpindi, a city in the northeast, cheer for their team at a cricket test, or match.

A young Sindhi girl wears a scarf, called a **dupatta***, around her head and shoulders.*

Pakistan was established as a Muslim **homeland**, and about 97 percent of its population is Muslim. Muslims practice the religion of Islam. They believe in one god, Allah, and his **prophet** Muhammad. Allah's commands, which were revealed to Muhammad by the angel Jibril, or Gabriel, are written in the *Qur'an*, the Muslim holy book.

Some Pakistanis live and work in sprawling cities, while others inhabit farming villages on the plains or in the mountains. People in each region practice their own customs and speak their own language. Many Pakistanis also speak English, the official language, and Urdu, the national language, which is used in many public schools and national newspapers. Major groups of Pakistanis include the Punjabis, Sindhis, Pathans, Baluchis, and Mohajirs.

Punjabis

Punjabis live in the province of Punjab, in cities and villages along the Indus River. They are the largest group of people in Pakistan, making up more than half the population. Many Punjabis farm the fertile plains of the region, but others play important roles in government, business, and the military.

The way of the Pathans

Pathans live in the North-West Frontier Province and in northern Baluchistan. They also live in Afghanistan, where they are called Pashtuns. They speak a language called Pushtu, or Pashto. Some Pathans live in large villages, towns, and cities, but others live in the northern mountains where they farm and raise animals. The Pathan tribes in the north run their own affairs, with little involvement from the Pakistani government. Elders, called the *kashar*, and a council made up of tribal leaders, called a *jirga*, make decisions and resolve disputes for Pathan tribes.

Baluchis

The Baluchis are the second largest group of people in Baluchistan, after the Pathans. They speak various **dialects** of Baluchi. Traditionally, Baluchis were goat and sheep herders who moved from place to place looking for water. After natural gas, coal, sulfur, and valuable minerals were discovered in Baluchistan in the 1950s, new roads and new people moving into the province began disrupting the Baluchis' traditional ways of life. Today, **nomadic** Baluchis live mainly in the northwest. Like the Pathans, they rely on a *jirga* to run their affairs.

Afghan refugees live in a camp near the border between Afghanistan and Pakistan.

Pathans follow a code of honor called **pukhtunwali**, *which means "way of the Pathans." As part of this code, Pathans seek* **badla**, *or revenge, for insults done to themselves, their families, or their tribes.*

Mohajirs

Mohajir means "refugee," or a person who leaves his or her country during a war or another dangerous time to seek safety in a new country. Mohajir was the name given to Muslims who came to Pakistan from India immediately after Pakistan became a country in 1947. Most settled in the city of Karachi in southern Sind, where they opened family businesses. Today, they make up two-thirds of Karachi's population and speak Urdu.

Afghan refugees

In 1979, the Soviet Union invaded Afghanistan. Over the next ten years, 3.3 million Afghan refugees streamed into Pakistan, mainly through the Khyber Pass. They lived in refugee camps near the border. Gradually, many moved away from the camps to find work in Pakistan's cities. Hundreds of thousands of Afghan refugees crossed into Pakistan in the months following October 7, 2001, when the United States and its **allies** began a war against **terrorists** in Afghanistan. They began to return to Afghanistan in 2002, once life there was a bit more peaceful.

Hotels, banks, travel agencies, and other businesses in the old section of Rawalpindi are located on a part of the Grand Trunk Road, which is a long highway that crosses the Indian subcontinent.

In 1947, the bustling city of Karachi became the first capital of Pakistan. By 1959, the government wanted to work in a city that was cooler, less crowded, and closer to other large cities. It moved the capital to Rawalpindi, in northern Punjab. Rawalpindi was only a temporary home for the government, until the new capital of Islamabad was completed a few miles away. Finally, in 1967, the government moved to Islamabad. Today, a busy highway connects Rawalpindi and Islamabad. The government plans to make the two cities one large "twin-city" that shares services.

The Empress Market, in the center of Karachi, was built by the British, who ruled Pakistan for about 200 years.

Karachi

Two hundred years ago, Karachi was a small fishing village on the shores of the Arabian Sea. Today, it is the largest city in Pakistan, where about ten million people live. Karachi is Pakistan's center of business and industry. Giant skyscrapers, steel mills, oil refineries, and factories where cars and ships are built rise throughout the city. Karachi is also one of the world's largest seaports. Enormous ships from Europe, the United States, and East Asia pack the harbor, along with smaller local fishing boats.

Islamabad

Workers began building Islamabad, which means "city of Islam," in 1961, near the cool, beautiful Marghella hills. Each section of the city has homes and parks that are built around a markaz, or commercial center with shops. White buildings, tree-lined streets, and large parks, including a garden with more than 250 types of roses, give the capital a peaceful atmosphere. One of the world's largest mosques, or buildings where Muslims pray, is in Islambad. The Faisal Mosque has room for 100,000 worshipers.

*Water from the Indus River is piped into wells in an area called the **Dhobi Ghat**, or "Great Laundry." Some people from Karachi come here to wash their clothes by hand. Then, they spread their clothes on hundreds of clotheslines to dry in the wind.*

The Faisal Mosque is made of marble, with a roof that looks like a gigantic desert tent. The mosque is named after King Faisal of Saudi Arabia, who paid for the mosque's construction.

🏔 Cities of the plains and frontiers 🏔

At the entrance to Lahore's old city stands the giant Delhi Gate. The walls of the gate are 20 feet (6 meters) thick, and the entrance is large enough to allow an elephant to pass through.

(top) Geometric and floral designs decorate the tombs of Sindhi leaders in Hyderabad.

Most of Pakistan's large cities, such as Lahore, lie near the Indus River or its tributaries. Lahore, which is the capital of Punjab and the country's second largest city, is often called "the heart of Pakistan." This modern city with shopping malls, computer stores, and high-end fashion boutiques was once the center of the Mughal Empire. The Mughals were Muslims who ruled parts of Pakistan and India for more than 200 years, beginning in the 1500s. They built the beautiful Shalimar Gardens just outside Lahore, as well as the Lahore Fort. The fort's high walls surround royal palaces, assembly halls, and an enormous mosque.

Hyderabad

In 1768, a Muslim ruler named Ghulam Shah Kalhora decided to build a fort on the banks of the Indus River. Its giant walls were 50 feet (15 meters) high. Some of these walls still stand at the center of Hyderabad, in the province of Sind. Hyderabad is the fourth largest city in Pakistan. Its bazaars, or markets, sell traditional Sindhi handicrafts, such as gold and silver jewelry, as well as glass bracelets. The tomb where Ghulam Shah Kalhora is buried was built into the hill on which the city sits.

A frontier town

In northern Pakistan, near the entrance to the Khyber Pass, lies the city of Peshawar. It is the capital of the North-West Frontier Province. For hundreds of years, invaders from Afghanistan and other parts of central Asia entered Pakistan through the Khyber Pass, settled in Peshawar, and built forts, tombs, mosques, monuments, and gardens. Travelers went to Peshawar's Qissa Khawani, or "Street of Storytellers," to tell people about their adventures. Today, people gather in the Qissa Khawani to eat in cafés or shop in bazaars. Beside the old city is a former British cantonment, where British troops trained and lived. The army camp in the cantonment is now used by the Pakistani army.

Gilgit

The Pakistani government controls the Federally Administered Northern Areas from the town of Gilgit. No other large town or city exists within 270 miles (450 kilometers) of this remote center. Gilgit is near the ancient Silk Road, which was a trade route people began using in the first century B.C. to carry silk from China into Pakistan. The town lies in a lush valley between the high mountains of the Karakoram Range. Although the mountaintops are white with snow throughout the year, apple and cherry orchards grow around Gilgit and bloom in spring and autumn.

Cars, carts, and people crowd the Qissa Khawani, in Peshawar, at the end of a busy shopping day.

Quetta

Quetta is the capital of Baluchistan and one of its few cities. Vineyards and apple and peach orchards surround the city, which lies in an earthquake zone.

Quetta is close to Pakistan's borders with Afghanistan and Iran. For hundreds of years, Pakistan's rulers used a fort in the city to guard the main roads against invading armies from these countries. The city's name comes from the Pathan word *kwatta*, which means "fort." Quetta remains a crossroads, or meeting place, for a large mixture of people. Pathans, Baluchis, Mohajirs, Punjabis, and Afghan refugees all share the city's streets and crowded bazaars.

Bazaars in Gilgit sell silk from China, as well as china, shawls, and the embroidered woolen caps worn in the region.

17

Outside Karachi are hundreds of sandstone tombs, known as the Chaukundi tombs. Carvings of leaves, flowers, and jewels decorate women's tombs, while horses and swords are carved onto men's tombs.

People have lived in cities and villages along the Indus River for thousands of years. Over time, soil and sand covered the early settlements, which **archaeologists** began to excavate at the beginning of the 1900s. West of the Indus Plain, they discovered Mehrgarh, one of the first farming villages in the world. People lived there between 7000 B.C. and 2000 B.C. Using mud bricks, the villagers built houses and granaries, where they stored barley and wheat. They also raised cattle and water buffalo to help with farmwork.

The remains of some early cities, such as Mehrgarh and Taxila, near Islamabad, have been named World Heritage Sites by the international organization UNESCO (United Nations Educational, Scientific, and Cultural Organization). UNESCO gives money to Pakistan to preserve and protect these sites, which are of value to the world.

Mohenjo-daro

Archaeologists have found the ruins of more than 300 cities from the ancient Indus Valley civilization, which lay along the banks of the Indus River. Mohenjo-daro, which means "Mound of the Dead," was discovered in Sind in 1922. Archaeologists found evidence that Mohenjo-darans grew wheat, barley, rice, fruit, vegetables, and cotton. They also raised sheep, goats, cattle, and chickens, and caught fish in the river. Human skeletons with holes in their teeth indicate that these ancient people practiced an early form of dentistry.

Mohenjo-darans lived in buildings made of red bricks. The bricks were baked in an oven called a kiln, not sun-dried like most other bricks were at the time. Many houses were two stories, and some even had bathrooms, with toilets connected to covered drains that ran down the streets. A wall surrounded important buildings, including public baths, an assembly hall, religious colleges, and royal palaces. Shops and houses stood outside the wall.

*A traditional dome-shaped **stupa** was built to store sacred objects at Mohenjo-daro. The **stupa** is on top of an ancient citadel, or fortress, where the rulers of Mohenjo-daro looked out over the entire city.*

Taxila

Cities have risen and fallen at Taxila for thousands of years. In the third century B.C., an emperor named Asoka took control of Taxila, and it became a center for his religion — Buddhism. Buddhists follow the teachings of a prince named Siddhartha Gautama, who became known as "the Buddha." "Buddha" means "Enlightened One." The Buddha believed that people could escape life's sufferings if they freed themselves of all desires, led truthful lives, resisted evil, did not hurt others, and respected all humans as equals. Taxila has the remains of Buddhist monasteries, where Buddhist **monks** lived, and rounded stone *stupas*, where holy items were stored. Archaeologists have found large and small statues of the Buddha throughout Taxila, including a stone statue called "the Healing Buddha." Worshipers believed that they would be cured of illnesses if they put their fingers in the statue's belly button.

An unsolved mystery

Although several million people were once part of the Indus Valley civilization, their cities were deserted by 1500 B.C. Archaeologists are not sure what became of the Indus Valley people. Some think that when the cities became too crowded, people left and returned to nomadic ways of life. Others believe that a change in climate dried the land. People were no longer able to farm, so they left the region because of a lack of food. Still others say that earthquake-like movements near Karachi raised the land along the coast. The Indus River could no longer reach the sea and instead flooded the interior, destroying the cities of the Indus Valley civilization.

Seals, which were probably used by governments, merchants, and guilds, or groups of tradespeople, were found at the Indus Valley city of Harappa. The seals have pictures of animals, such as bulls, elephants, and unicorns, as well as pictorial symbols written from right to left. No one has been able to decipher the writing yet. It is unlike the writing of any other ancient people.

A sculpture at Taxila shows the Buddha meditating with his eyes half shut. The long, stretched earlobes on the sculpture are a sign of the heavy, rich jewelry that the Buddha wore.

The crops of Punjab and Sind

When Pakistan was still part of India, the region of Punjab was called "the Granary of India" because so much grain grew in its fertile soil. Today, farmers across Punjab still grow grain, including wheat and rice, as well as sugar cane, tobacco, cotton, vegetables such as potatoes, cabbage, and cauliflower, and fruits such as mangoes, grapes, pears, and peaches. Farmers in Sind harvest similar crops, but are especially known for their guavas, bananas, oranges, and lemons.

Pakistan's warm weather allows farmers in some regions to harvest two crops each year. *Kharif*, or summer, crops are planted from April to September and harvested from October to March. They include rice, sugar cane, cotton, and corn. *Rabi*, or winter, crops are planted from October to January and harvested from April to June. They include wheat, tobacco, barley, and animal feed, such as hay.

A Pathan woman milks a goat while her son holds its horns to keep it still.

More than half of Pakistanis live and work on farms, where they grow crops or raise cattle, goats, sheep, and chickens. Workers on larger farms use modern machines and chemical **fertilizers** to grow crops that are sold all over Pakistan and in other countries. People who live on smaller farms grow enough to feed their families and to sell a little in the village market. They often do farmwork by hand, using simple tools instead of machines. Many farmers are tenant farmers, or sharecroppers, who rent land from someone else. Over the past 40 years, the Pakistani government has taken some land away from wealthy landowners and given it to tenant farmers so they can own the land that they farm.

Bales of sugar cane are processed to make sugar, molasses, and a delicious juice. Fibers from the plant are used to make paper.

Workers at a cotton mill in the eastern city of Bahawalpur scramble on top of a pile of cotton bolls to fill their sacks. The cotton bolls will later be washed and made into fabric.

Steps of crops

Giant steps look like they climb the sides of mountains in northern Pakistan. These "steps" are really terraces that farmers cut into the mountains so they have flat fields on which to grow mulberries, walnuts, apricots, wheat, barley, corn, and potatoes. Stone walls hold each terrace in place, and tall rows of poplar and birch trees protect the crops from strong winds. The crops are watered by *nalas*, or little streams of water from melting glaciers. Some crops are dried on the rooftops of valley homes. During the apricot harvest, the roofs look orange, and during the mulberry harvest, the roofs look white and purple. The north is also known for its fertile valleys filled with orchards where apples, peaches, cherries, figs, plums, and pears grow.

Cotton

Pakistan is the perfect place to farm cotton plants, which only grow in warm, dry climates. One-tenth of the world's cotton comes from farms on the Indus Plain. The white cotton fibers are found inside round seed pods, called bolls. The fibers are sold to other countries or spun into cotton thread, much of which is then woven into cloth on machines called looms.

The wheat harvest

After golden stalks of wheat are cut from fields in Pakistan, they are laid on the ground and crushed by oxen who walk in a circle on top of them. The oxen's heavy hoofs crush the wheat until it becomes a heap of straw, husks, and seeds. Farmers toss the crushed wheat into the air with wooden forks. The wind blows away the chaff, or straw and husks, leaving the heavy seeds, or grains, to fall back on the ground. Then, the seeds are collected in sacks and ground into flour.

The lush Hunza Valley lies between rocky mountains. The steep ground has been cut into terraces for farming. Different crops can be planted on each terrace.

The flat, sunny roofs in the village of Altit, in the Hunza Valley, are a perfect spot to dry large baskets of apricots.

Fishing

Fish from the Arabian Sea, as well as trout farms in the north, provide food and income for many people in Pakistan. Large fisheries sell fish to other countries, while people in small fishing villages catch enough to feed their families. The Makrani people live along Baluchistan's coast, where for hundreds of years they have caught shrimp, sardines, and sharks in the Arabian Sea. They dry their catches in the sun before selling them in markets.

About 25,000 people, called the Mohana, rely on the fish of Manchhar Lake in Sind. Many Mohana live in houses on the shore or on small islands in the lake, but some live in boat colonies, in intricately decorated houseboats. They fish from smaller boats, or they train birds called herons to catch fish for them. Unfortunately, the Mohanas' fishing traditions and ways of life are disappearing. **Sewage** and chemicals from factories are being dumped into the lake, killing many fish.

A Mohana family rests on their houseboat on Manchhar Lake. The boat's flat roof provides shelter from the sun and rain, and is used as a storage area for extra blankets and supplies. The smaller boat is used for fishing.

A woman pumps water from a well outside Peshawar. In some rural areas, people walk for miles to reach a source of fresh water.

Farmers on the Indus Plain water their crops with the help of irrigation. Wide irrigation canals carry water from the Indus River and its tributaries into each village. There, the canals empty into narrow, brick-lined ditches or metal pipes, called tube wells, which carry water to each field. Electric pumps in tube wells push the water through the pipes. The irrigated pieces of land between ditches and pipes are called *doabs*. The *doabs* of the Indus Plain make up the largest area of irrigated land in the world. Irrigation canals remove so much water from the Indus River that large boats can no longer travel on most parts of the river.

An irrigation system waters the crops on a terraced field near Karimabad, in the Hunza Valley.

Water from stone

The dry, cracked plains of northern Baluchistan are not very fertile, but people there still grow rice, onions, and fruits, such as apples and peaches. They use a special irrigation system called *karez*. Rainwater is collected in underground canals at the bottom of rocky hills. The canals carry the water to fields that are sometimes 12 miles (20 kilometers) away. The canals slope upward near farmers' fields so water can exit the ground. In Quetta, *karez* water empties into a large, cool underground cavern, where people collect the water in buckets. Transporting the water underground prevents it from evaporating in the hot, dry air. Large holes leading into the canals are dug every 50 feet (15 meters). Once a year, people crawl down the holes to clean dirt and sand from the canals.

On this farm in Sind, the rising water table brought salt to the surface and destroyed the rice crop.

Too much water

On some farmland, the problem is not too little water, but too much. Heavy rains and floods cause irrigated land to become waterlogged, meaning it cannot soak up any more water. The level of underground water, called the water table, is rising in Pakistan, carrying salts from deep in the earth to the surface. Many crops cannot grow in the salty soil. Two-thirds of the farmland in Sind is already waterlogged.

Cattle graze on a waterlogged field in Punjab. There is so much water that crops can no longer grow on this land.

Saving the soil

To dry out waterlogged farmland, large plastic pipes are buried underground. Excess water in the ground drips through holes in the pipes and is carried to rivers and lakes. Farmers also plant trees that need large amounts of water, such as poplar and eucalyptus, around their fields to soak up the moisture. When the trees get large, they are cut down and sold to paper mills. For land that cannot be dried out, scientists in Pakistan are developing a type of wheat that will grow in salty soil.

Many industries in Pakistan manufacture products from crops that farmers grow and from animals that they raise. Factories turn wheat into flour, sugar cane into sugar, and oil seeds into cooking oil. Craftspeople working in homes and small factories create leather goods from animal hides and sew beautiful designs into cotton with cotton thread. Raw cotton, cotton thread, and cloth are Pakistan's most important **exports.**

Made in Pakistan

Glass, telecommunications equipment, surgical and dental instruments, and cement are all produced in Pakistan. Steel mills rise near Karachi, where workers in a Suzuki factory assemble cars and vans made from Japanese parts. Factories in Karachi and Lahore turn raw cotton into cotton cloth, sheets, clothes, and bedspreads. Sports equipment made in the city of Sialkot, in northeastern Punjab, is famous around the world — especially field hockey sticks, tennis rackets, and cricket bats.

This factory in Mirpur Mathelo, in eastern Sind, manufactures fertilizer for Pakistan's many farms.

The Tarbela Dam is the world's largest dam made of earth. It took eight years for 15,000 workers to build.

Water power

At enormous dams along the Indus River, water flows through huge turbines, or motors, that generate hydroelectricity. Hydroelectric power is the main source of energy in large towns and cities around the Indus River. The Tarbela Dam provides hydroelectricity to the people of Islamabad and Rawalpindi. Its reservoir, which is more than 48 miles (80 kilometers) long, also provides people with drinking water and water for irrigation.

In mountain villages, the water from melting glaciers provides another source of hydroelectricity, although not a reliable one. Electricity in these villages depends on the heat of the sun melting the glaciers. Villagers often have poor electricity for most of the year and no electricity in the winter when the glaciers do not melt. It is very common to hear people calling out *"Bijli chattam,"* meaning "Power is off."

(above) *A worker pours molten metal in a Karachi steel factory. Steel from Karachi is used in industries such as shipbuilding and car manufacturing.*

Digging deep

Many valuable minerals, metals, and sources of energy lie under the ground in Baluchistan. Across the province, people mine coal, copper, iron ore, sulfur, gold, and bauxite, which is used to make aluminum. Pipes carry natural gas from the Sui field in eastern Baluchistan to Karachi, Hyderabad, Lahore, and Rawalpindi, where the natural gas powers industry and is used as fuel for cooking and heating in homes.

A mineral called onyx is mined in Nagundi, near Quetta. Miners blast open the ground with dynamite to find large chunks of onyx, which they cut into smaller pieces with sharp saws. The onyx looks like marble, and is white, brown, green, or a mix of colors. Craftspeople shape the onyx into many items, from beautiful carvings to coffee tables.

Salt

More than 600 million years ago, a sea that flowed over northern Punjab dried up, leaving white and pinkish-red streaks of salt in the ground. Today, this area, called the Potwar Plateau, has some of the largest salt mines in the world. Salt has been mined at the city of Khewra for 500 years. The mines are huge caves, with clear pools of water and stalactites. Stalactites, which look like enormous icicles hanging from the roofs of caves, form as salty water drips from the ground above.

(below) Miners at the Khewra salt mines load trolleys with blocks of reddish salt. The Khewra salt mines are the second largest source of salt in the world.

Small, colorful pieces of cotton cloth are sewn together to make a quilt in the artform known as **rilli**.

Sindhi textiles

Artisans in Sind have made textiles for so long that even ancient Greek literature refers to "Sindon cloth." In bazaars throughout Sind, people sell reversible cotton bedspreads called *khais*, cotton shawls for men called *ajraks*, white woolen blankets called *khatos*, and cotton cloths decorated with bright stripes called *sousis*. To make patchwork quilts, shawls, and rugs, people use an artform known as *rilli*, which is a combination of printing, embroidery, and appliqué, or sewing one piece of fabric onto another.

Leather

Craftspeople in Baluchistan and Sind use leather to make many items, including vases and traditional slippers with curled toes. They also make lampshades by stretching camel skin over a clay mold and painting it with bright colors. The skin is translucent, so once it is placed over a light bulb, light shines through it and the colors glow.

Hundreds of soccer balls crowd a factory in Sialkot, which is the world's largest soccer ball manufacturer.

Art on wheels

Trucks and buses covered in brightly painted designs make their way down many Pakistani streets and highways. Paintings of flowers, landscapes, movie stars, and politicians, as well as mirrors, sequins, lines of poetry, and religious sayings, decorate the vehicles. The drivers sometimes hire artists to do the work because the most beautifully painted trucks and buses often get the most business. Customers believe that people who take good care of their vehicles are also safe drivers.

Sometimes called motor rickshaws, scooter rickshaws, or tuk-tuks because of the sound their engines make, some cities have banned these vehicles because they are very loud and cause a lot of pollution.

City streets in Pakistan hum with cars, taxis, motorbikes, and buses that are sometimes so full that passengers sit on the roof. People also pay rickshaw drivers to give them rides. Rickshaws are three-wheeled motorized vehicles with a canopy on top. The driver sits on a seat in the front and steers the rickshaw with handlebars, like a motorcycle. Two or three passengers sit on a bench in the back.

Along with the sound of motors, some Pakistani streets echo with the clip clop of animal hoofs. Horses pull passengers in two-wheeled carts called *tongas*. Horses also pull carts with heavy loads down old, narrow streets, as do cattle, donkeys, and camels.

Every surface on this Pakistani bus is decorated. Even the driver's seat is covered with embroidered cloth.

The highest road in the world

The Karakoram Highway (KKH) winds from the foothills of the Karakoram Range through the mountain's icy peaks to Pakistan's border with China. It is the highest tar road in the world, rising to 15,528 feet (4,733 meters) at the border with China. The KKH is part of a highway system that begins in Islamabad and ends in Kashgar, a city in China. Built between 1966 and 1986, the highway system created a trade route between Pakistan and China, and made it easier for people in northern Pakistan to communicate and trade goods with people in the center of the country. The highway system also connected isolated villages in the north. Until the late 1970s, people from these villages had very few roads, so they walked for days to reach another village or town.

On the mountains around the Karakoram Highway, landslides happen almost daily and avalanches are common. During the highway's construction, avalanches and falling boulders killed 7,400 people. These people are honored with memorials on the side of the highway. Workers with shovels patrol the highway in pick-up trucks to clear away piles of mud and rocks, while bulldozers wait every 20 miles (32 kilometers) to clear away larger messes. Unlucky travelers must sometimes stop for a day or two until the road ahead of them is cleared.

All aboard!

The British began building a railway system in Pakistan more than 100 years ago. Today, tracks link many major cities and towns in the country. Most trains run on diesel oil, but older steam trains still puff along some tracks. Steam trains usually have only one engine, but a very special steam train takes tourists through the Hindu Kush Mountains. This steam train needs two engines, one at each end, to climb the steep mountain slopes.

A steam train connects Baluchistan's remote towns. Pakistan is one of the few countries that still operates steam trains. Some trains are more than 70 years old.

Some people call snow leopards "clouded leopards" because the smoky spots on their pale gray fur look like clouds.

Pythons and crocodiles swim off the coast of Pakistan, while the blind Indus River dolphin navigates by **sonar** through the Indus River delta. Very few wild animals live on Pakistan's dry plains and deserts, except for foxes, bats, jackals, small rodents, and reptiles, such as the Indian spiny-tailed lizard. In southern Punjab, blackbucks, antelopes called blue bulls or *nilgai*, and gazelles called *chinkaras* live in Lal Suhandra National Park. Most of Pakistan's wildlife can be found in the northern mountains. Here, dense forests of oak, chestnut, eucalyptus, and pine trees shelter musk deer, big-horned Marco Polo sheep, wild goats such as markhors and ibexes, and snow leopards.

Purring leopards

Snow leopards prowl through the snowy northern mountains, with thick hair on their tails and on their paws to keep them warm. The leopards' color allows them to blend in to the snow-covered, rocky landscape when they sneak up on ibexes, Marco Polo sheep, and other prey. Today, snow leopards are **endangered** because hunters kill them for their fur. Only 250 leopards now roam in Pakistan's mountains.

Caring for the land

As forests are cut down and plants in waterlogged, salty soil die, the places where Pakistan's animals live are vanishing. This loss, combined with overhunting, means entire species are becoming **extinct**. The government has established national parks to protect pieces of land and the animals that live there. For example, Khunjerab National Park is near Pakistan's border with China. It shelters snow leopards, Himalayan ibexes, wolves, and the rare Marco Polo sheep.

When Khunjerab National Park was established in 1975, it included land where people from surrounding villages had raised yaks, sheep, and goats for more than 400 years. People in the village of Shimshal worried that the park would destroy their way of life, and they refused to keep their animals from feeding there. Today, the Shimshalis are trying to convince the government that their traditional way of life protects the environment, and that they should keep control of their grazing lands.

Markhors are endangered because people hunt them for their unusual twisted horns.

Jasmine grows wild in Pakistan. It is also cultivated in the beautiful Rose and Jasmine Garden in Islamabad.

Birds of many feathers

More than 600 types of birds fly through Pakistan's skies, including kites, crows, and magpies. The huge bearded vulture, which has a wingspan of nearly ten feet (three meters), lives in the mountains. Its very unusual diet consists of the bones of dead animals. If the bones are too large to eat, the vulture drops them from a high place so they shatter into smaller pieces.

In the Thar Desert, the male sandgrouse uses his breast feathers to carry water to his nest. Tiny hairs on the feathers hold the water while he flies. At the nest, young birds squeeze the wet feathers with their bills to drink. Another desert bird, the Houbara bustard, flies up to 24 miles (40 kilometers) a day to find water. The bustard is now endangered because of overhunting.

Growing in a dry country

The dry, hot summers in most parts of Pakistan make it difficult for anything taller than grasses or short bushes to grow. Khejri trees survive in the Thar Desert because their long roots soak up water from deep underground. People who live in the desert use the leaves of these trees to feed their goats and camels and to make tea. In Baluchistan, only xerophytic plants, or plants that grow in hot, dry climates, survive, including the ephedra, which is used to make medicines for asthma, bronchitis, and other lung diseases.

Jasmine

Many kinds of jasmine bloom across Pakistan, in formal gardens and in the wild. Mughal emperors first planted these white or yellow flowers throughout their elegant gardens. Jasmine is now Pakistan's national flower. With its sweet, fruity smell, it is used to flavor tea and make perfumes. People also believe that the jasmine's scent calms them when they are upset.

Glossary

ally A country that helps another country, especially during a war

archaeologist A person who studies the past by looking at buildings and artifacts

delta An area of low flat land where a river divides into several smaller rivers before flowing into the sea

dialect A way of speaking that differs from the standard form of the language in its words, sayings, and pronunciation

endangered Describing an animal or plant that is at risk of being destroyed

export A good sold to another country

extinct No longer in existence, as with dinosaurs

fertile Able to produce abundant crops or vegetation

fertilizer Material added to soil to make it produce more crops

homeland A country that is identified with a particular people or ethnic group

lagoon A shallow body of water connected to a large body of water

mangrove trees Tropical trees that are held high above the water by their tangled roots

monk A member of a male religious community who has taken vows, such as silence or poverty

nomadic Having no fixed home and moving from place to place in search of food and water

plateau An area of flat land that is higher than the surrounding land

prophet A person who is believed to speak on behalf of God

sewage The waste from homes and businesses that passes through sewers and drains

sonar The detection of objects using sound waves

subcontinent A large landmass that is part of a continent, but is considered independent

terrorist People or organizations that use violence to further a specific cause or to intimidate people or government

torrent Very fast-moving water

tributary A river or stream that flows into a larger river or a lake

Index

    1 2 3 4 5 6 7 8 9 0   Printed in the USA   0 9 8 7 6 5 4 3 2